AF270517

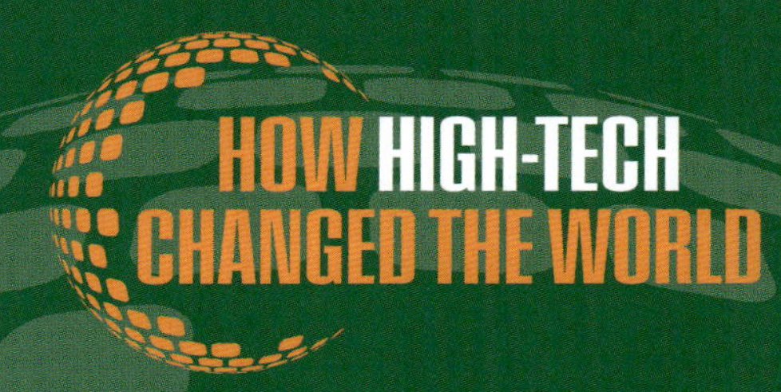

NETWORKS

Published in 2025 by **Cheriton Children's Books**
1 Bank Drive West, Shrewsbury, Shropshire, SY3 9DJ

© Copyright 2025 Cheriton Children's Books

First Edition

Author: Kelly Roberts
Designer: Paul Myerscough
Editor: Jennifer Sanderson
Proofreader: Amy Strauss
Consultant: David Hawksett, BSc

Picture credits: Cover: Shutterstock/Trong Nguyen (t), Shutterstock/Albert89 (c), Shutterstock/Monkey Business Images (l), Shutterstock/TunedIn by Westend61 (b).
Inside: p4: Shutterstock/Antonio Guillem, p5: Shutterstock/Hywards, p6: Shutterstock/GaudiLab, p7: Shutterstock/Dean Drobot, p8: Shutterstock/Rawpixel.com, p9: Shutterstock/Tint Media, p10: Shutterstock/Metamorworks, p11: Shutterstock/Asharkyu, p12: Shutterstock/Fizkes, p13: Shutterstock/Feng Yu, p14b: Shutterstock/KPhrom, p14t: Shutterstock/Metamorworks, p15: Shutterstock/Panuwat Phimpha, p16: Shutterstock/Photosince, p17bl: Wikimedia Commons/Stansfield PL, p17br: Wikimedia Commons/Steve Jurvetson, p18: Shutterstock/Daniel Krason, p19b: Shutterstock/Photosince, p19t: Shutterstock/Casimiro PT, p20: Shutterstock/Monkey Business Images, p21: Shutterstock/BritCats Studio, p22b: Shutterstock/Dennizn, p22t: Shutterstock/Ground Picture, p23l: Wikimedia Commons/Veni Markovski, p23r: Wikimedia Commons/Veni Markovski, p24: Shutterstock/Everett Collection, p25b: Shutterstock/Everett Collection, p25t: Shutterstock/Fizkes, p26: Shutterstock/Tero Vesalainen, p27: Shutterstock/Ivan Marc, p28: Shutterstock/Jacob Lund, p29: Shutterstock/NicoElNino, p30: Shutterstock/Oneinchpunch, p31: Shutterstock/Drserg, p32: Shutterstock/Antonio Guillem, p33: Shutterstock/Anthony Correia, p34: Shutterstock/NDAB Creativity, p35: Shutterstock/Neeraz Chaturvedi, p36: Shutterstock/Northfoto, p37: Shutterstock/GaudiLab, p38: Shutterstock/Linda Moon, p39: Shutterstock/Fizkes, p40: Shutterstock/McLittle Stock, p41: Shutterstock/KateV28, p42: Shutterstock/Zamrznuti Tonovi, p43: Shutterstock/Frederic Legrand/COMEO, p45b: Shutterstock/Albert89, p45t: Shutterstock/Frederic Legrand/COMEO.

Printed in China

Please visit our website,
www.cheritonchildrensbooks.com
to see more of our high-quality books.

CONTENTS

THE NETWORKS STORY

Today, networks are all around us. They give us power, connect us to the world, and provide us with entertainment. Thanks to networks, we can check emails on a cell phone, play games with people miles away, watch live sports on television or on the Internet, and be connected to friends at the touch of a button.

A System of Communication

The first system to use electricity to transmit messages over huge distances was the electric telegraph. The first electric telegraph line opened between Washington D.C. and Baltimore in 1844. The electric telegraph allowed people to send messages in the form of words spelled out using short bursts of electrical noise. This system was named Morse code, after its inventor, Samuel Morse. After the invention of the telegraph, people could communicate with others on opposite sides of the world, forever changing global business and politics.

Without a network connection a smartphone loses many of its useful functions, such as its ability to stream movies.

Complex and Simple

The technology needed to create today's high-tech networks is very complicated, but the principles behind it are simple. Networks connect things, be it electrical power lines, telephone cables, or computers. Networks have existed for many years, but it is only in the last 200 years that they have revolutionized our lives. For example, hundreds of years ago, there were simple postal networks for sending and receiving letters. However, it was only in the 1900s that these networks became widespread and accessible enough for everyone to use.

A Technology That Changed the World

Computer and entertainment networks are the systems that allow people to send and receive communications, and share data. With networks, it is now possible to remotely connect computers around the world—and this "information technology" age has changed the way we live. In this book we'll explore the history of networks, how they have changed your world, and the brilliant scientists behind this world-changing invention.

HOW HIGH-TECH CHANGED THE WORLD

We rely on networks to live our day-to-day lives. Keeping in touch with friends and family, whether by using cell phones, email, letters, or the Internet, would not be possible without high-tech networks. We would not be able to buy the things we want using one click of a mouse, have groceries delivered, or pay electricity bills over the phone. Without networks, we would not even have old-fashioned fixed-line telephones.

Connecting to Others

We use many different networks in our everyday lives. Some connect us to electronic devices in our homes, while others help us communicate with the rest of the world. Before learning how computer networks work, it is important to learn about the many different types of network and what they do.

The Network Around Us

The most basic network is the one that exists around us. This network is the connections that enable our personal electronic devices, such as computers, printers, smartphones, and music players, to communicate with each other. For example, at home you may have a desktop computer that is connected to a printer, or a musical keyboard, using a Universal Serial Bus (USB) cable. The computer may also be connected to a modem, which in turn allows you to access the Internet. From time to time, you may also connect your smartphone to the computer to copy over music or movie clips. This simple network of electronic devices is known as a personal area network (PAN).

Cables or Wireless

When you print a document or download photographs, you are using your PAN. Any electronic devices you plug into your computer using a cable are part of this personal network. Instead of using traditional wires, devices in your personal area network can also be connected using wireless technology, such as Bluetooth or Wi-Fi. These use invisible radio waves used to send and receive information.

HIGH-TECH HISTORY

The first Bluetooth device, a hands-free headset for cell phones, was unveiled at an electronics show in 1999. Two years later, the first cell phone that included Bluetooth was available for people to buy. Bluetooth is a wireless technology that allows electronic devices, such as ear pods, smartphones, and computers, to share, send, and receive information over very short distances, around 32 feet (10 m) at best. The information, or data, is sent, received, and shared between Bluetooth devices using invisible radio waves.

Bluetooth is a perfect wireless format to connect the increasing number of smart devices that we keep on our person, such as phones, earbuds, and smart jewelry.

Connecting More than One Computer

A PAN usually contains just one computer. If you want to connect a number of computers, you need to set up a local area network (LAN). There are millions of LANs all around the world. Some, such as those used by schools, colleges, and businesses, connect a lot of computers in the same building. This enables these computers to share resources, information, and access to the Internet. However, LANs need not be this big. If you have two or more computers in your home, and they share a single Internet connection, then you are using a simple LAN.

Connecting to a LAN

At home, your LAN may be wirelessly connected using Wi-Fi technology. However, for a large LAN with several computers, such as a LAN in a library or office building, the computers will be connected using wires called Ethernet cables. One of the main tasks of most LANs is allowing people to share computer files. Many large LANs do this by using a central storage computer, called a server. All the computers in the network will be connected to the server (see pages 18–19). Some people use their LAN to play games with their friends. For many years, PC gaming enthusiasts have hosted "LAN parties," with up to 20 people playing against each other, over one local area network, in a large room or garage.

A fraction of a second difference in pressing a button can mean success or failure when online gaming, so a good Internet connection is needed for a player to be competitive.

HOW HIGH-TECH CHANGED THE WORLD

Ethernet cables were invented in 1980 to allow speedy connections between several computers or devices in a LAN. The cables work by breaking large amounts of data into tiny "virtual packets," called frames. These frames can then be sent from one computer to another in the same LAN in just a fraction of a second. This transformed the speed at which data could be shared.

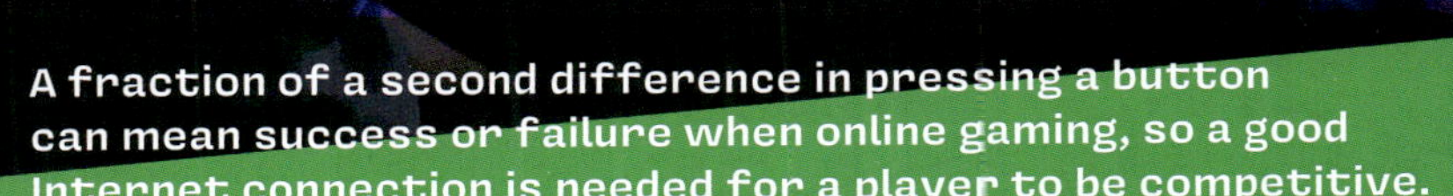

Connecting the LANs

LANs connect computers in a small area, usually inside the same building. A network that connects a number of different LANs over a larger area is called a metropolitan area network (MAN).

Metropolitan Connection

According to the Institute of Electrical and Electronics Engineers (IEEE), the organization that decides on worldwide communications standards, a metropolitan network can vary in size from a few blocks or a cluster of buildings to an entire city. The largest MANs can be up to 30 square miles (70 square km) large. However, most MANs are smaller than this and are roughly the size of a large university campus.

A World-Wide Gateway

Many businesses and large organizations, such as local councils and police forces, use MANs to securely connect LANs in different buildings and locations. This means that instead of connecting fewer than 100 computers, they can potentially connect thousands. The main point of MANs is to connect small LANs to what is known as the wide area network (WAN)—the worldwide network of cables that carries computer communications around the world. MANs are our gateway to the World Wide Web (WWW).

The term "information superhighway" refers to the Internet, WWW, and other digital forms of communication.

Ethernet cables are used in LANs, MANs, and WANs, and have been in use since the early 1980s. They use traditional wire cables as well as fiber-optics.

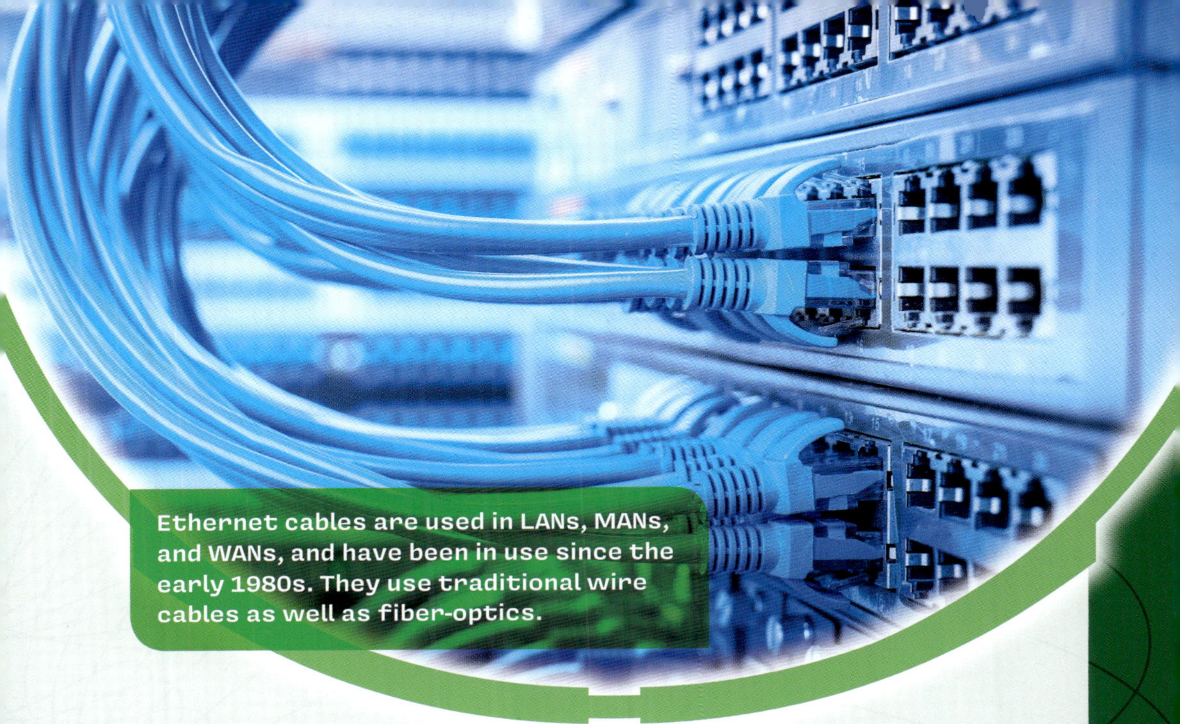

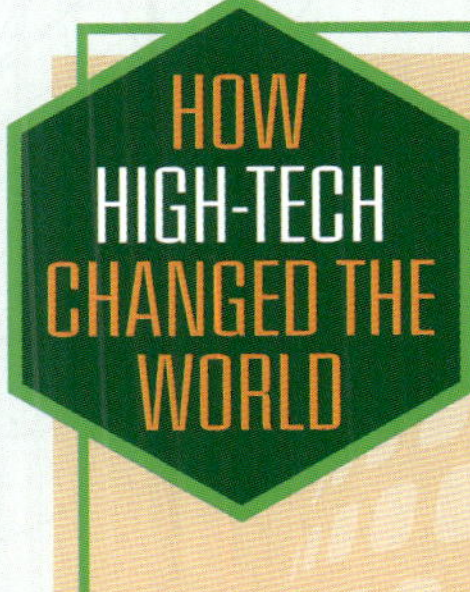

Data Delivery

Today, most computer communications between LANs and MANs are carried along special fiber-optic cables. These cables turn computer data into pulses of light, which can travel down the fiber-optic cables at incredibly fast speeds. At the other end of the cable, the pulses of light are then turned back into data that a computer can understand.

HOW HIGH-TECH CHANGED THE WORLD

Making glass into fiber was first achieved by the Romans in around 27 BCE, but it was only after the invention of the laser, in 1960, that glass fibers became a possibility for global communications. Today, the Fibre-optic Link Around the Globe (FLAG) connects 28 countries with around 17,398 miles (28,000 km) of optical fiber cables on the ocean floor. There are now more than 400 submarine cables that use optical fibers with a total length of around 800,000 miles (1.3 million km). Optical fiber has made global networking possible.

Modern Internet speeds are powerful enough to support real-time video calls with many participants.

Connecting the World

The wide area network (WAN) is the system of fiber-optic cables, telephone cables, and communication satellites that connects every country on Earth. It is what allows us to phone friends overseas, check emails, surf the WWW on our smartphones, and play games against people in other countries.

A Mighty Network

The WAN is a global series of smaller (but still enormous) connected networks. Some of these networks are the size of whole countries, while others are as big as entire regions or states. Together, they connect everyone to the wider world.

How It Works

The WAN is a like a communications transportation system. Just as the interstates, freeways, railroads, and airplane routes allow us to travel around the country, and the world, the cables and satellites of the WAN allow telephone calls, television shows, and computer data to do the same. Using the same transportation example, your local MAN is like the bus, train, or subway services that allow you to move freely around your hometown or city. But to go farther, you need to connect to the WAN.

Networks Connect Networks

Every time you connect to the Internet, or you use a computer to send an email to someone, you are connecting to the WAN. You connect to the network through the other three networks —PAN, LAN, and MAN. Connecting to the WAN is done in just millionths of a second, without you even noticing.

HIGH-TECH STARS WHO CHANGED THE WORLD

GARY THUERK

On 3 May 1978, Gary Thuerk, an employee of computer company Digital Equipment Corporation (DEC), sent the first-ever unsolicited mass email. It was a promotional message for the company's latest computer. He sent it to 393 people using the Advanced Research Projects Agency Network (ARPANET), the predecessor to the Internet. In 1978, only 393 people in the world had an email address—and Thuerk sent his email to them all. It was the first-ever spam. Although the introduction of spam nearly half a century ago was not popular, Thuerk had changed the way the Internet was used forever.

Today, our email services are constantly updated to spot spam emails and put them in a separate folder.

CHAPTER 2

UNDERSTANDING NETWORKS

We have seen how the different types of high-tech network allow us to connect to, and communicate with, the world around us. But how do these networks really work? Data, in the form of electrical signals, light, or sound, is transported around the world using fixed cables or through the air via radio waves.

How Things Connect

For a network to work properly, it must decide whether to connect using cables or wirelessly—using radio waves. Some networks use just one method, while others use a combination of the two. Both do the same thing in different ways. Systems that use cables turn data, sound, or pictures into electrical signals (or, as in the case of fiber-optic cables, light), which then travel down wires to their destination. At the other end, the signals are then turned back into data, sound, or pictures. This is the system used by fixed-line telephone networks, cable television, and most computer networks.

Using Radio Waves

Today, more networks use radio waves to transmit the same information over long distances. This is how cell phone networks operate, how satellite television works, and how we can connect wirelessly to the Internet using Wi-Fi. Radio waves are invisible waves of energy that can travel enormous distances. However, radio waves are not as reliable at sending data as cables, which is why cell phone calls often break up, and the picture on satellite television services looks grainy during periods of bad weather.

What Affects Waves?

Radio waves do not actually fail but, because they are sent through the air, they can be affected by the weather and other services that use similar technology. Different types of network use different lengths of radio wave to transmit information. Radio waves that only need to travel short distances are less likely to fail.

HIGH-TECH HISTORY

Wi-Fi stands for "wireless fidelity," and is the result of many inventions in the 1990s by different companies around the world. A Wi-Fi router broadcasts a short-range "bubble" of radio waves, allowing devices to connect to the Internet without cables. In 1999, Apple released their iBook laptops, the first mass-produced device to include Wi-Fi, beginning the demand for wireless devices worldwide. Today, all smartphones, tablets, and computers come with Wi-Fi, as well as other devices, including smart watches.

Many public places now have free Wi-Fi. Sometimes, a free W-Fi service will show you an advert to support the cost of running a free service.

When YouTube was launched in 2005 it changed the way people watched videos. People could "stream" videos directly from YouTube's servers without having to download them first.

Sending a Request

Every second of each day, huge amounts of information flow through the cables and wireless services that power our networks. This information takes the form of hundreds of millions of individual requests. They could be to fulfill a task, such as sending an email, or for specific information—for example, carrying out a WWW search on a search engine such as Google.

Clients and Hosts

The different requests flow between "clients" and "hosts." The client is the person using a particular piece of technology to access the network. For example, this device could be a laptop computer or a smartphone. The host can be either the place where the information is stored, such as the computer that stores a particular website, or the company that provides the service, such as a cell phone network provider or the Internet service provider.

Interactions Everywhere

In our day-to-day lives, we make a huge number of client-host requests. Every time we make a phone call, watch a video on websites such as YouTube, post things to social media sites such as Facebook, or download an MP3 file, we are requesting, and receiving, information from a host. It does not stop there. When you switch on a light at home, you are making a request to the electrical power network. It is the same if we switch on a gas oven or buy a ticket for a trip. Client and host interactions are all around us.

Handling Millions of Requests

Tthe world's most popular search engine, Google, requires a huge number of super-size host computers, called servers, to handle the enormous number of Internet search requests it receives every day. According to experts, Google uses more than 2 million servers to power its online services.

HOW HIGH-TECH CHANGED THE WORLD

Google was created by Larry Page and Sergey Brin while they were students at Stanford University, California. They named their search engine after a misspelling of the number googol, which is a 1 followed by 100 zeroes. Google is now the largest search engine in the world and is the most visited website. In 1998, two years after its launch, Google processed around 10,000 searches each day. Today, it handles around 8.5 billion searches daily. The search engine has transformed how people search for information on the WWW.

The video clips that we watch on our smart devices are stored in enormous banks of information called servers.

What Are Servers?

Servers are the huge, incredibly powerful computers that act as hosts. They handle hundreds of millions of individual network requests every day. Without these supercomputers, most networks on which we rely would not work.

A Specific Task

Servers are not like normal computers. As well as being hundreds of times more powerful than an average home computer, they are usually designed to do just one specific task. This could be storing web pages or media, such as the video clips on YouTube and the music files we download, or performing a specific task, such as allowing us to send and receive emails. Every time you connect to the Internet, you access servers.

When you send an email, your computer will make a connection to your Internet service provider's mail server. Before the recipient receives the email, they will have to access the service provider's mail server to download the message.

Servers in Smaller Networks

Servers are also used in much smaller networks, such as the LANs used in schools or offices. Here, the server is usually used as a place to store documents that can be accessed by many different computer users at the same time. These could include coursework notes, company accounts, or other important paperwork.

Backing Up

Servers are so important to big Internet companies such as Apple, Amazon, and Google that their systems include a huge number of back-up servers. This means that if they receive more requests at the same time than their regular servers can handle, additional requests will be rerouted to the back-up servers.

Amazon has evolved to be an enormous online store that sells almost anything, from clothes to food.

HOW HIGH-TECH CHANGED THE WORLD

Amazon and eBay both launched in 1995, just one year after the world's first online retail transaction. eBay began as a site to allow individuals to sell to each other, and now has more than 130 million users who regularly buy goods. Amazon began as an online bookstore that expanded to include anything that can normally be purchased in a physical store. In just a couple of decades, Amazon and eBay have completely changed the way we shop.

Amazon has produced so much wealth for its founder, Jeff Bezos, that he now has his own space program!

Keep the Data Flowing

With billions of network requests every day, it is important for those who run networks to put in place technology that helps information flow freely. In today's computer networks, this is done using hubs, switches, and routers.

What Is a Network Hub?

A network hub is a box into which you can plug a number of network devices, such as computers and printers. The devices are linked to the hub using Ethernet cables (see page 9). In a school, office, or college campus, the network hub links together the devices in a LAN. Usually, it will also allow each of these computers to access a single, shared link to the Internet.

Switching Networks

Network switches are used to ensure that requests reach their intended target. This could be a particular computer, web service, or Internet server. Large Internet companies, such as Amazon and Google, also use switches to manage the amount of requests they receive. If a particular server gets more requests than it can handle, a network switch will push the request to a back-up server.

What Are Routers?

Just as junctions help cars and trains switch between roads and tracks, routers allow information to pass between different networks, or different parts of the same network. Routers are vital to the flow of information. They ensure that requests from client computers reach their intended destination.

Linking to the WAN

Today, most people connect to the Internet at home using a router. A router enables a number of smartphones, different computers, and smart TVs to share a single Internet connection. They "route" all the different network requests, or traffic, providing a link to the WAN.

HIGH-TECH HISTORY

Before the Internet was the Advanced Research Projects Agency Network (ARPANET). In the 1960s and 1970s, computers were still in their infancy, and many of the most powerful computers were at universities. Researchers from all over the United States wanted to use these computers, and ARPANET allowed them to do so without needing to travel to the universities that hosted them. The computers were large mainframe devices that programmers used a terminal, with a keyboard and screen, to access. ARPANET allowed people to use different computers from any terminal that was connected to the network.

This home router is linked to the Internet via the blue cable, which connects to a broadband wall socket. The red and gray Ethernet sockets can connect computers and printers, but they can also be connected by using the router's Wi-Fi bubble.

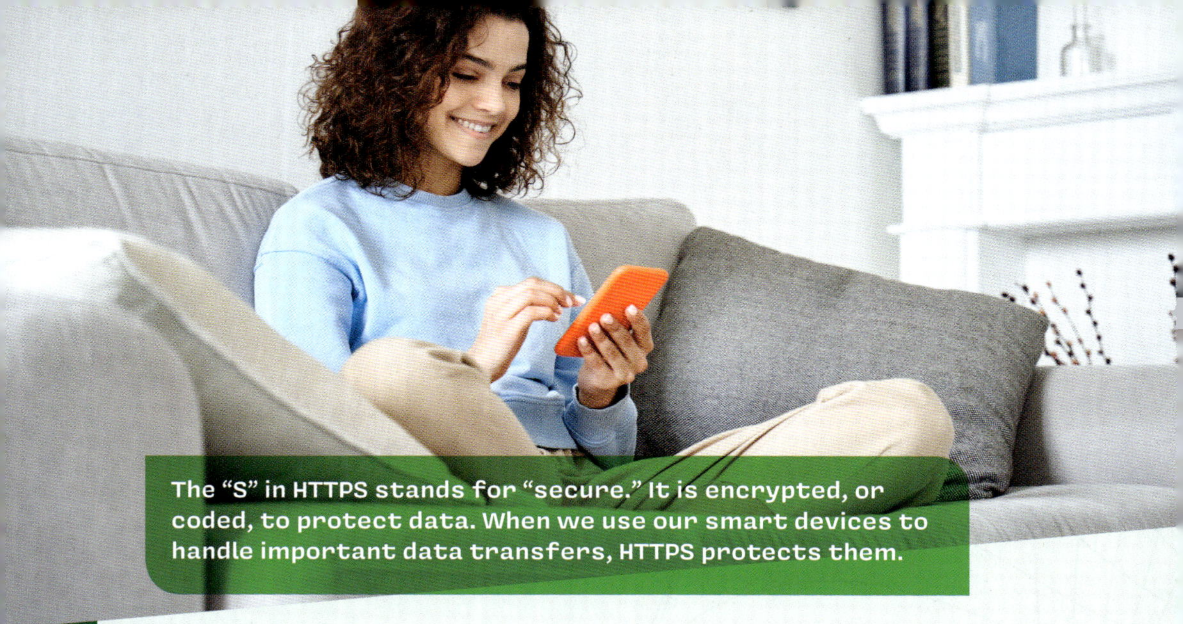

The "S" in HTTPS stands for "secure." It is encrypted, or coded, to protect data. When we use our smart devices to handle important data transfers, HTTPS protects them.

What Are Protocols?

We now know how information moves around networks and the different technology used to make that happen. But how is the data organized as it flows around the world? In order for computers to communicate and for information to reach its intended target, networks use a set of rules. These rules are known as protocols. Protocols establish how information passes through the Internet. Without protocols, you would have difficulty reading a particular website.

A Specific Job to Do

Each protocol allows us to do a different task. For example, a Hypertext Transfer Protocol (HTTP) allows us to read websites. Transfer Control Protocol (TCP) and Internet Protocol (IP) ensure that we can connect to the correct host server to retrieve information or send and receive emails. Even simple tasks, such as surfing the web, require your computer to follow a number of protocols at the same time. Because of this, protocols are usually stacked up in layers. Just as it may take more than one filling to make a sandwich, it can take many layers of protocols to perform one network request.

Without protocols, we would not be able to access websites such as Wikipedia.

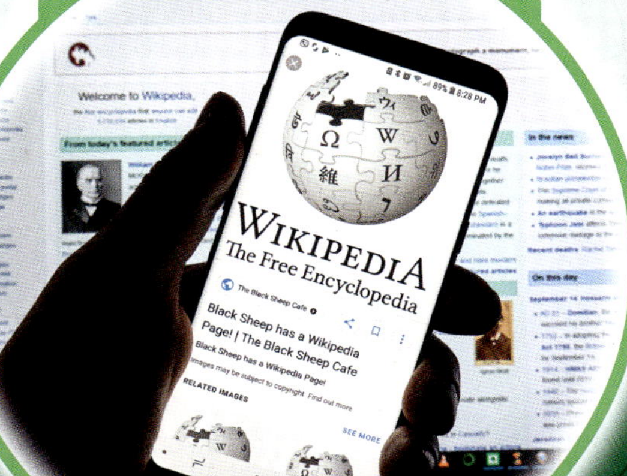

Seven Layers Needed

According to computer scientists, most networks use seven layers of protocol to send and receive information. The definition of each of these layers is incredibly complicated. Each layer is concerned with a specific part of the process, from the cables carrying the information to how it is displayed on a computer screen.

HIGH-TECH STARS WHO CHANGED THE WORLD

BOB KAHN AND VINT CERF

Vint Cerf is an engineer who, along with his colleague, Bob Kahn, created the TCP and IP protocols that are one of the most important parts of the Internet. Cerf and Kahn worked on ARPANET, which used a system called "packet-switching." An old-fashioned telephone conversation requires a specific connection between callers to last the duration of the call. Packet-switching allows everything in a message to be split into many parts that can reach its recipient independently, without a single, dedicated connection. This was a revolutionary invention, and for that reason, Vint Cerf and Bob Kahn are known as the "fathers of the Internet."

NETWORKS PAST AND PRESENT

Modern communications networks are incredibly complicated and capable of sending and receiving huge amounts of data. But it has not always been this way. Little more than 150 years ago, it was impossible to speak to someone in a neighboring town without traveling to see them. So how did the current network communication age come about?

Bell and the Telephone

In 1876, a Scottish scientist named Alexander Graham Bell filed patent papers for an invention that allowed two people in different places to talk to each other. Bell realized that, using a capable device, it was possible to send and receive sound using electrical wires. The telephone, as the device became known, was a revolutionary idea. Over the next 100 years, a network of cables carrying telephone lines began popping up all around the world, connecting people in different towns and countries. These connections were made possible by the cables themselves and by telephone exchanges.

The early telephone network relied on human operators working at telephone exchanges. They used a system of cables and sockets to physically connect a call to its recipient.

Sending a Signal

Telephone exchanges worked on the same principle used by today's network routers. For example, if you call someone who lived on the other side of the world, the electrical signal sent by your telephone passes along a series of cables to a local exchange. At the local exchange, it is diverted to an international exchange to begin its journey across oceans and continents. National and local exchanges at the other end of the line then push the signal toward its intended destination.

HIGH-TECH HISTORY

Alexander Graham Bell (1847—1922) did not get his telephone to work until three days after his patent was granted. Its first successful use was a "call" from Bell to his assistant, in which he asked, "Mr Watson, come here—I want to see you." Watson clearly heard Bell from his device in a different room, and came to him. It was a turning point in technology history.

Using Radio Waves

Following the development of early telephone networks, it was not long before scientists discovered that it was possible to transmit sound through the air using radio waves. It was a discovery that paved the way for an entertainment revolution.

The Revolution of Radio

The principle behind radio is similar to that of telephone systems. Like the telephone, radio uses a transmitter and a receiver. The transmitter converts sound into electrical signals that can be broadcast as radio waves. The receiver then picks up the signals and converts them back into sound. At first, scientists struggled to get radio waves to travel more than a few miles, but, eventually, they built larger, more powerful transmitters capable of broadcasting over hundreds and even thousands of miles.

Sending Pictures

Soon, scientists realized that moving pictures could be sent through the air in a similar way. Like radio, the pictures and sound could be broken up into electrical signals for transmission. The receiver (in this case a television set) then turns these electrical signals back into sound and pictures. Television was even more revolutionary than radio. Networks of television transmitters were built to relay television signals around the world. The networks are the television equivalent of Internet routers or telephone exchanges.

Streaming a Show

Today's cable television services use Internet network technology to make watching television more interactive. Using technology similar to client-and-host services, viewers can watch television shows on demand, order pay-per-view movies, and even choose different camera angles on live sports broadcasts.

HOW HIGH-TECH CHANGED THE WORLD

Before streaming services and smart TVs, people had to watch a show at the time that it was broadcast. Their only alternative was to record it onto a VCR cassette, to watch later. Streaming video content over the Internet became possible when MPEG-4 was developed. In 1998, an international agreement by the Moving Picture Experts Group (MPEG) allowed the video format to be used, and the video to be compressed so that it could be easily streamed by home users. The age of streaming had arrived.

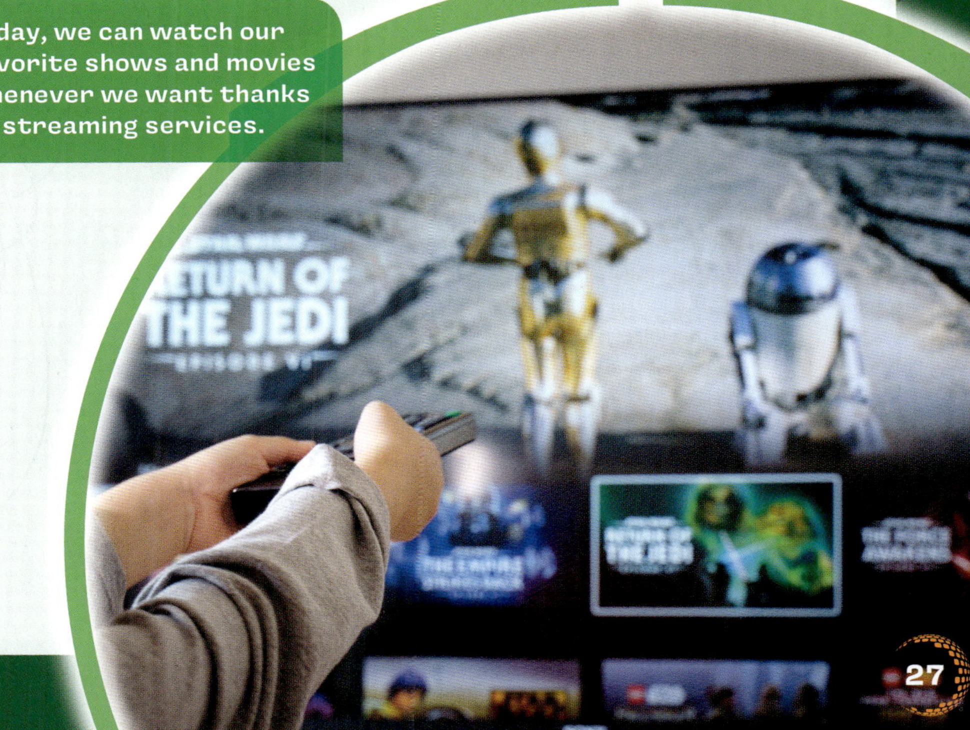

Today, we can watch our favorite shows and movies whenever we want thanks to streaming services.

Using Wi-Fi to log-in to a library's network can let you browse its entire collection and even tell you exactly where each book is located.

Connecting Computers

Ever since the first computers were built by scientists in the 1950s and 1960s, the race was on to connect them. But it took almost 50 years for international computer connections to become commonplace.

Building a Modem

Early computers were very large and expensive. Only governments, universities (most of whom built their own), and large international companies could afford them. Despite the expense, the world's few computer users wanted to link them together so that they could share information. In 1962, computer scientists at the telephone company AT&T built the world's first modem. It was capable of sending computer data using ordinary telephone lines. Establishing a connection between two modems was done in a similar way to making a telephone call—the user had to dial the number of the modem with which they wished to communicate. Although primitive, the modem would later drive the Internet revolution.

ARPANET to Internet

After the invention of the modem, a number of cutting-edge developments pushed the boundaries of computer networks. In 1964, the American company IBM built the world's first telephone ticket reservation system for American Airlines. This system used computers to connect American Airlines offices in 64 cities. In 1970, computers at four universities were connected using telephone lines to create ARPANET. The idea behind it—to allow computers in many different places to easily exchange information—became the basis of the Internet.

The ARPANET paved the way for the exchange of digital messages in the form of emails (see below).

HIGH-TECH STARS WHO CHANGED THE WORLD

RAY TOMLINSON

In 1971, a computer science researcher named Ray Tomlinson (1941–2016) sent a short message, made up of just a few random letters, over the ARPANET network. At the time, the network was used by only the US military. This message would go down in history as the world's first email. Before this achievement, electronic messages could only be sent to, or left for, people who used the same computer as the sender. Ray decided to use the @ symbol, between someone's name and their machine or location. The addition of the @ resulted in an email, and we use the symbol today in all emails.

An International Network

Computer researchers and scientists had hoped for an international network that could connect people in countries around the world for a long time. Yet until the 1980s, this was just a pipe dream.

Overcoming Problems

There were many problems that had to be overcome before computer users around the world could easily communicate. The biggest problem during the 1970s and early 1980s was that although the number of computer networks was increasing, most of these were not connected to one another. There was no common set of rules, or protocols, and very little way for people outside large universities or government agencies, such as the National Aeronautics and Space Administration (NASA), to use the system.

Making the Rules

The "international network" came a step closer in 1982. Researchers at ARPANET and the Defense Advanced Research Projects Agency (DARPA) worked together to decide on a set of protocols for international computer networking. The system they created, which included TP and IP, is still used today.

A New Network Age

From the early 1990s onward, the Internet grew rapidly. Companies called internet service providers began to sell access to the Internet to home computer users. Anyone with a computer could join the Internet revolution. The new network age had truly begun.

Today, it's difficult to imagine a world without the Internet.

The WWW

In 1989, a British scientist named Sir Tim Berners-Lee created a system for sharing text and pictures over the Internet. He called this system the World Wide Web (WWW). Berners-Lee encouraged people around the world to use the WWW and create their own websites. The idea caught on, and today, there are more than 1 billion websites!

HIGH-TECH STARS WHO CHANGED THE WORLD

SIR TIM BERNERS-LEE

Sir Tim Berners-Lee is a British computer scientist best known for being the inventor of the WWW. Berners-Lee was working at CERN (the large particle accelerator experiment in Geneva on the France-Switzerland border) when he proposed a way of using the infrastructure of the Internet to host a gigantic hypertext document system. The system would allow anyone to access information that was connected with links. Berners-Lee created the URL system and the HTTP protocol still used today. The WWW's first use, in the early 1990s, was as an online telephone directory for scientific staff at CERN.

When out of any Wi-Fi range, a smartphone's cellular network connection can keep you online. However, streaming high-quality video, such as movies, over the cellular network uses a lot of data.

No Computers Needed

Thanks to wireless technology such as Wi-Fi, today it is possible to access the Internet without using a computer. Amazingly, it is also possible to read web pages and send emails using the same cell phone network you use to make a call.

First for the Public

The first public cellular phone network was set up in Chicago in 1977. It allowed people to make calls on cell phones, which sent and received signals using radio waves to a network of masts placed around towns and cities. The first cellular telephones were used in the United States in 1946. They were effectively large radios, and were so big that they had to be fitted inside cars. Carphones, as they became known, were of limited use and expensive. Despite this, carphones remained in use until the 1980s.

Networks Today

Today's cellular network, so called because it divides the nationwide network into a series of small grids or cells, is far more advanced than the one set up in the 1970s. Each cell has its own mast, and each mast is given a unique radio frequency to send and receive calls. As users pass from one cell to the next, their cell phone will automatically detect the change and tune in to the new frequency.

Supersmart Phones

Smartphones such as the iPhone are capable not just of joining the cellular network, but also of accessing the WWW using Wi-Fi. Wi-Fi also uses radio waves, but is capable of handling much larger amounts of data than the cellular network. This makes it possible to watch live television or listen to the radio on your phone.

HIGH-TECH HISTORY

Although the cellular grid system is very stable, it can fail if it is overloaded. This happens when too many people in one cell area try to access the grid to make calls at the same time. That famously happened in New York City in the hours following the 9/11 terrorist attacks in 2001.

In 2001, cell phone networks were far less advanced than they are today. When the Twin Towers of the World Trade Center collapsed, the thousands of people trying to contact loved ones overloaded the networks.

CHAPTER 4

MODERN NETWORKS

The technological and scientific advances of the last 100 years have not only changed the way we communicate forever, but also the way we work, study, manage our money, and spend our leisure time. Without modern networks, our lives would be very different—networks have transformed modern living.

Simple and Effective

The greatest network the world has ever seen is the WWW. When we think about going on the Internet, what we usually mean is accessing the WWW. It is a vast network of individual websites containing all kinds of information, resources, and services. The genius of the WWW is its simplicity. Using a special piece of computer software called a browser, we can visit hundreds of millions of websites, all in a matter of seconds.

The WWW has transformed the way that students carry out research.

Finding the Answer

Before the invention of the WWW, it was much more difficult to find information. For example, today, if you want to read about the lives of the presidents of the United States, you can find detailed histories online in seconds. Before the WWW, you would have had to go to your local library to find a book about the presidents. Whatever you are interested in, you will find information on the web. You can read newspaper articles, look up flight timetables, check your bank balance, and find out what is showing at a local movie theater. The WWW puts the world at your fingertips.

A Website Host

Each website is stored, or hosted, by an individual computer or server. The website will have its own unique address, called a URL. This enables people to search for the website online. When you type the site's address into your web browser and press return, your computer is actually connecting to the computer or server that hosts the website.

HOW HIGH-TECH CHANGED THE WORLD

YouTube is the online video-sharing platform that rapidly changed how people share video content. Launched in 2005, it allows people to upload, share, like, dislike, and comment on videos. It allows anyone to become their own television channel and to also stream live video, as well as upload. In 2023, the most popular YouTube search word was "song," with "movie" coming second.

At the start of 2024, India had the most YouTube users—at least 462 million! The United States was second, with 239 million users.

Data Sharing

Today, one of our favorite pastimes is sharing things with friends online, from photos and videos to songs. We also share important information, such as work-related data or legal documents.

Moving Data

Sharing online, be it uploading home movies to websites such as YouTube or TikTok, or putting your vacation photos on Instagram, is possible only because of the advances in network technology over recent years. In the early days of the Internet, people connected using ordinary telephone lines that could carry only small amounts of information, quite slowly. Today's fiber-optic and broadband cables can transport enormous amounts of information incredibly quickly.

Not Good for Everyone

Those who use and rely on filesharing sites believe they are a force for good. Those inside the music and movie industries may not agree. Movie and music executives have seen their profits fall as more people illegally swap songs and movies online. The first online file-sharing service to clash with the entertainment industry was MP3-sharing service Napster.

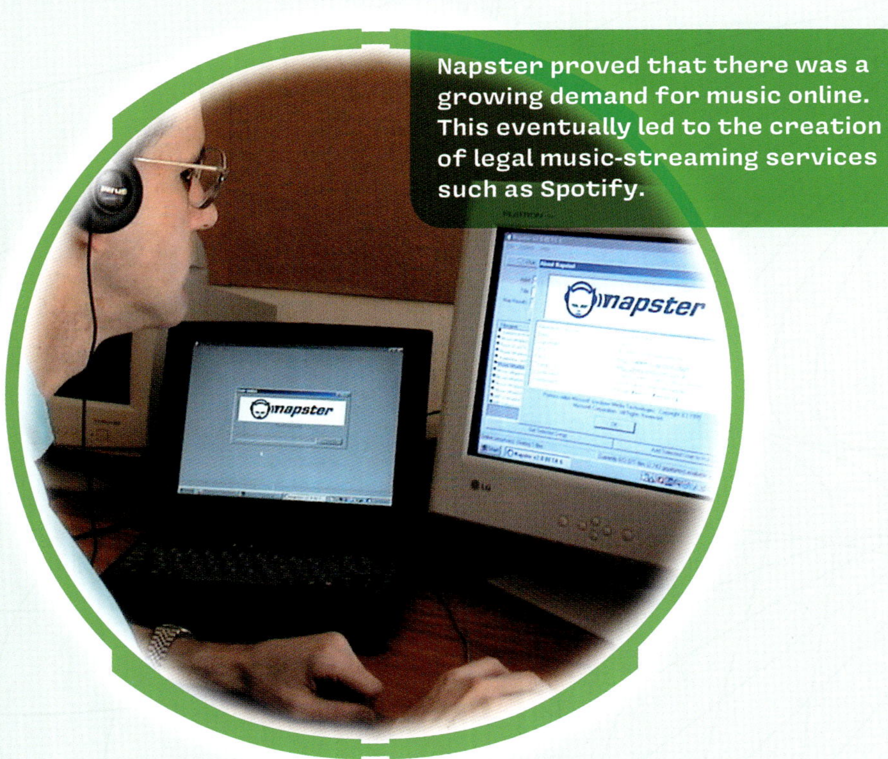

Napster proved that there was a growing demand for music online. This eventually led to the creation of legal music-streaming services such as Spotify.

Sharing with Friends

Napster was one of the first file-sharing services to use a free technology called peer-to-peer (P2P) networking. Napster's cutting-edge software allowed users all over the world to download MP3 files from other users without paying for them. Today, illegal file sharing using P2P networks is as popular as ever, despite the efforts of the entertainment industry to shut down these services.

HOW HIGH-TECH CHANGED THE WORLD

Unlike regular networks, which use the "client-and-host" system, storing information on dedicated servers, P2P networks do not use a dedicated server. Instead, each computer on the network acts like a mini server, with files (MP3s, movies, and so on) that can be accessed by all the other users on the network. Illegal downloading of movies, television shows, video games, and music has grown since Napster's debut in 1999. A recent study showed there were 215 billion visits to piracy websites worldwide in 2022. Of these visits, 13.5 billion were from people in the United States, with television shows being more in demand than any other media.

The first smartphone to include a camera was released in 2000, but the camera was very basic. Today's phone cameras can take professional-quality images, which can easily be shared on sites such as Instagram.

Keeping in Touch

Not so long ago, we used phones and standard postal services to keep in touch with friends and family. Now, thanks to modern communications and computer networks, we can chat with the world 24 hours a day. Social networks such as TikTok and Instagram have revolutionized the way people keep in touch with one another. They are called social networking sites because, although they are based around websites, they act like a network, connecting us with friends, family, and acquaintances.

Connected with Video

Another great advance is video conferencing, such as Zoom and Skype. These services allow you to make video calls using your laptop, tablet, cell phone, or a computer connected to a webcam. Such services are a new version of old-fashioned television technology, with a little bit of Internet magic thrown in. Because they do not rely on old-fashioned telephone networks, calls cost much less than regular phone calls. In fact, video calls to other registered service users are free.

Using Skype, you can make calls to other Skype users for free over the Internet or a cellular network. This is made possible because Skype mixes two types of network technology: P2P networking and client-server. When you make a call, the service uses the Internet to connect you directly to the other person's computer or smartphone, rather than the telephone or cellular networks.

Keeping Connected

Zoom began in 2012, as an app that allowed up to 15 people to be in the same video call. A month after launch, 400,000 people were using Zoom. The increase in working from home due to the Covid-19 pandemic saw a huge rise in the app's popularity—it was downloaded 2.13 million times in March 2020 alone. Zoom allowed people to keep connected with family, friends, and coworkers during times of lockdown. Since then, many more people have begun to work from home thanks to the success of the technology.

Video conferencing allows people to hold online meetings while working from home. The increase in working from home has resulted in less commuting, which is beneficial for people and the environment.

Changing How We Relax

The network revolution brought about by fiber-optic cables and the worldwide spread of the Internet has not just changed the way we keep in touch—it has also changed the way we have fun and spend our free time. The speed of modern-day fiber-optic cables and their ability to carry huge amounts of data at once have made it possible to do many things online that would previously have been impossible. You can now watch high-definition television shows and movies on your computer, play online games against people in different countries, and watch your favorite sports teams from the comfort of your home.

Ordering Online

Before the Internet Age, shopping was something people had to plan into their days. They would have to drive to the mall, or take the bus or subway into town. Today, there are so many online stores that you can shop from the comfort of your own home. Whatever you want to buy, from clothes and electrical goods to music and groceries, you can find it online and have it delivered to your door—often at cheaper prices than in local stores.

Today, there are many services and apps that can automate your order so that your favorite food arrives at your door at the same time each week.

Great Gaming

Online gaming is a great example of a client-server relationship. The game players are the clients. They connect over the Internet to the gaming network's server. This server responds to the instructions or requests from the players. It tracks the game and displays the action on computers or game consoles at record speed.

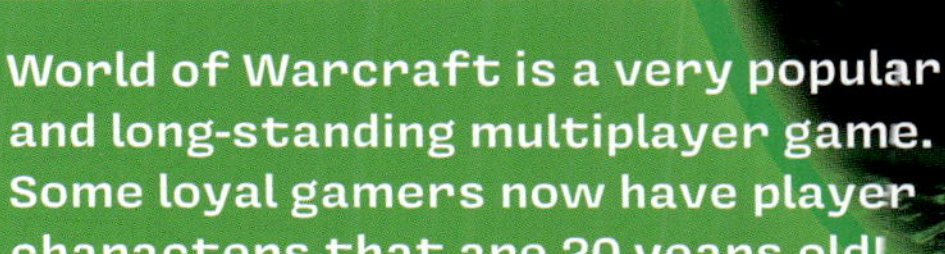

World of Warcraft is a very popular and long-standing multiplayer game. Some loyal gamers now have player characters that are 20 years old!

HOW HIGH-TECH CHANGED THE WORLD

World of Warcraft is an online game with around 129 million players worldwide. Launched in 2004, it is one of the most successful online games of all time. In 2005, a software error introduced a disease that rapidly infected the player characters of many users. Panic spread among players, and some who had characters with healing abilities went to the major cities to act as first responders. The behavior of players was so interesting that the US Centers for Disease Control and Prevention (CDC) studied the World of Warcraft accidental pandemic to learn how people would behave if a real pandemic, such as Covid-19, took place.

Closed Networks

Not all networks can be accessed by anyone. In fact, even in this age of mass global communication, there are still many secret or closed networks that can be accessed only by a select few computer users.

Secret and Safe

Closed or secret networks are networks that allow access only to a limited number of people. Most are classified as secure networks, which means that they are protected by security measures such as passwords or other special computer software. Many governments use closed networks to keep sensitive information, such as that used by the police or secret services, inaccessible to terrorists. However, occasionally, information from these secure networks becomes public. This is what happened when the WikiLeaks website made public thousands of secret communications between officials in different countries.

Keeping Private

Not all closed networks are secretive. Many companies, schools, and colleges routinely set up their own private network to securely share information and resources. A private network that can be accessed only by those in a specific institution is known as an intranet. Another good example of a closed network is the system of automatic teller machines (ATMs) operated by banks for clients to withdraw and deposit cash. Although the ATMs are all connected to computer servers, for security purposes they are not connected to the Internet at large.

Hidden Networks

In recent years, a number of hidden networks have been created to allow anonymous Internet users the chance to buy and sell things that are illegal, such as drugs and stolen goods. The most famous of these controversial and illegal networks was "The Silk Road," an online marketplace similar to eBay. The network was finally shut down in 2014 by the combined forces of the Federal Bureau of Investigation (FBI) and Europol.

HIGH-TECH STARS WHO CHANGED THE WORLD

MARK ZUCKERBERG

Mark Zuckerberg is the cofounder of Facebook. While studying at Harvard University, Mark and his friends launched Facebook, but made it available only to people studying at certain universities in the United States. This limited access made the website desirable, but it was eventually removed and anyone was allowed to join. By 2012, Facebook's number of users had grown to 1 billion and by the end of 2023, more than 3 billion people were on the site and using it at least once a month.

A HIGH-TECH FUTURE

Networks are all around us, enhancing our lives and enabling us to communicate with each other wherever we are in the world. While we are aware of many of the networks we use each day, there are others that are vitally important but we may not even realize that we are using them. Most of these networks are based on cutting-edge satellites positioned high above Earth. These send and receive data via radio waves and huge transmitters on the ground. The global television news coverage we take for granted is possible only thanks to this network of space satellites. The same can be said for the Global Positioning System (GPS), the satellite network that powers car navigation systems, keeps flights on track, and allows people to use Google Maps on their smartphones to find their way.

Making Networks More Secure

As we move deeper into the twenty-first century and networks become ever more advanced, fears increase for their security. Governments spend billions of dollars every year on network security to stop criminals and terrorists from stealing our money or bringing the world to its knees. So far, there have been few major disasters caused by network security failures, but some experts think it will only be a matter of time before one happens.

A Future of Superfast Connection

At present, only 66 percent of the world has access to the Internet. By 2050, experts think the Internet will be available, in one form or another, to everyone on the planet. They also say that connection speeds in the United States will be hundreds of times faster than they are today!

The lack of infrastructure is why not all people are connected to the Internet and the WWW. Many rural communities in very poor countries are not connected with fiber-optic cables, but the solution to this problem is coming from space. Many companies now operate satellites in space that, with the right receiver, can provide a connection to the Internet to anyone on the ground. The most famous is Elon Musk's Starlink constellation of satellites, which is intended to provide global satellite Internet access.

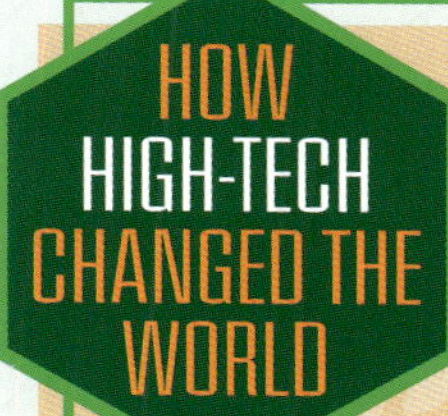

Elon Musk is the billionaire mastermind behind one of the latest network advances—Starlink.

Starlink already has more than 5,000 satellites, and this number is set to rise to at least 12,000. That will make networks available to many more people around the world.

GLOSSARY

acquaintances people you know, but who are not friends or family

Bluetooth a wireless system that allows cell phones and other devices to communicate with each other

broadband an Internet connection that can transport far more information than a traditional telephone line

communication the exchange of thoughts, opinions, or information

computer data information sent and received by computers or similar electronic devices

data information

download to transfer something from the Internet onto your personal computer or smartphone

Ethernet a type of cable used for connecting, or networking, computers

fiber-optic cables cables made up of many long, thin strands of plastic or glass

Internet a network of smaller computer networks that join to form a single global network

intranet a computer network that can be accessed by only a small number of people

millisecond one-thousandth of a second

modem a device that allows computers to send and receive information over the telephone network

protocols rules

radio waves invisible waves of energy that can pass through the air

satellite a device sent into space for a specific purpose, for example, enabling communication

server a supercomputer designed for a specific task, for example, storing information or running a network

software a computer application or program designed to do a specific task, for example, send email, edit photos, or record music

transmit to send information

transmitter a device that transmits, or sends, information, often in the form of radio waves or electrical signals

Universal Serial Bus (USB) a type of wired connection between devices to transmit data and power

upload to transfer something from your computer to a website or Internet server

webcam a small video camera that connects to your computer and allows you to send or receive video messages or live-stream from your computer

website a collection of writing, pictures, music, and sound that is stored on a computer and made available to everyone on the WWW

Wi-Fi a system that allows computers and cell phones to connect to computer networks without a traditional system of cables

wireless technology that allows the exchange of information but does not require wires

World Wide Web (WWW) the global network of websites

FIND OUT MORE

Books

Oxlade, Chris. *Computer Science for Curious Kids: An Illustrated Introduction to Software Programming, Artificial Intelligence, Cyber-Security—and More!* Arcturus, 2023.

Shofner, Melissa. *Computer Network Architect* (Behind the Scenes with Coders). Rosen Publishing Group, 2018.

Small, Cathleen. *How to Choose Your Perfect Computer Science Career* (STEM Career Choices). Cheriton Children's Books, 2023.

Tanenbum, Andrew, *et al. Computer Networks.* Pearson Education, 2021.

Websites

For more information on the Internet, log on at:
https://kids.britannica.com/kids/article/Internet/353293

Learn how cell phones work at:
https://kids.kiddle.co/Mobile_phone

Publisher's note to educators and parents:
All the websites featured above have been carefully reviewed to ensure that they are suitable for students. However, many websites change often, and we cannot guarantee that a site's future contents will continue to meet our high standards of educational value. Please be advised that students should be closely monitored whenever they access the Internet.

INDEX

ABOUT THE AUTHOR

Kelly Roberts has written many children's science and technology books. It's thanks to network technology that she was able to write this book (and have some downtime streaming movies)!